TO

First published in paperback in Great Britain in 2006 by HarperCollins Children's Books
HarperCollins Children's Books is a division of HarperCollins Publishers Ltd.

1 3 5 7 9 10 8 6 4 2

ISBN 13: 978-0-00-724144-6

ISBN 10: 0-00-724144-5

The HarperCollins website address is: www.harpercollinschildrensbooks.co.uk

Printed and bound in China

Why I Love Christmas

Illustrated by Daniel Howarth

HarperCollins *Children's Books*

I love Christmas because...
it's cosy inside.

I love Christmas because...
we have fun with our friends.

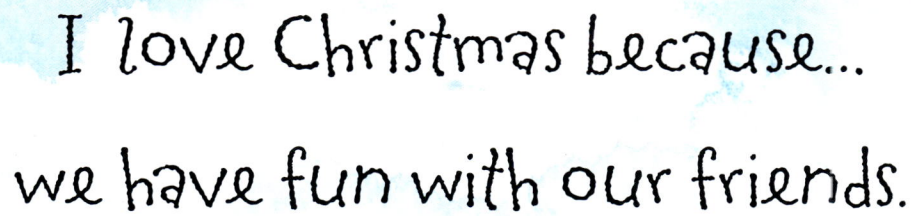

I love Christmas because...

we hide our presents.

I love Christmas because...
we sing songs.

I love Christmas because...
we make colourful decorations.

I love Christmas because...
we play games.

I love Christmas because...

the moon
is bright.

I love Christmas because...
our friends and family come to visit.

I love Christmas because...
we tell stories.

I love Christmas because...
there is lots to eat.

I love Christmas because...
everyone takes naps!

I love Christmas because...
there are extra kisses
and cuddles for everyone.

I love Christmas because...
we have parties!

everyone is happy.

Merry Christmas.

Stick a picture of
yourself here.

Love from